THE
VANISHING
COWBOY

THE VANISHING COWBOY

PHOTOGRAPHY BY
JIM AND CHRIS BERTOGLIO
TEXT BY DR. JIM HOY

TATE PUBLISHING
AND ENTERPRISES, LLC

Published by Tate Publishing & Enterprises, LLC
127 E. Trade Center Terrace | Mustang, Oklahoma 73064 USA
1.888.361.9473 | www.tatepublishing.com

Tate Publishing is committed to excellence in the publishing industry. The company reflects the philosophy established by the founders, based on Psalm 68:11,
"The Lord gave the word and great was the company of those who published it."

Book design copyright © 2015 by Tate Publishing, LLC. All rights reserved.
Cover design by Samson Lim
Interior design by Gram Telen

Published in the United States of America

ISBN: 978-1-63367-588-9
History / United States / State & Local / West (AK, CA, CO, HI, ID)
15.07.07

In memory of
Albert James "Jim" Bertoglio
(1925–2012)

FOREWORD

"How did you get the idea for this photo shoot, anyway?" I ask as I'm served a delicious glass of peach iced tea. I'd come to the Bertoglio home seeking answers, and Chris and his mom, Jan, were more than accommodating. Like prior conversations, the answer to my question would invariably center on a name and life that seemed to have started it all: Jim Bertoglio.

Born in 1925, and given his first camera eleven years later, Jim's view of life would be captured behind the lens of a camera. His lifelong talent in black-and-white photography was inspired by Ansel Adams, his instructor and mentor. During his six months of intensive training at the LA Art Center school, Jim demonstrated a high degree of accomplishment for one so young. When drafted in 1943, he was highly recommended by both the school and the acting chief of the Signal Corps liaison section for military assignment as a professional photographer.

During his nineteen months overseas (1944–1945), Jim served in Eddie Rickenbacker's 94th Aero Fighter Squadron, the oldest Air Force squadron in the US Air Force. Jim documented the life of fighter squadron pilots and ground crews that kept sixteen Lockheed P-38s airborne and in combat during the last months of the war. His photographs were sent by wire to the United States for publication and, once home, had prints made and framed for exhibit from negatives he had saved.

Following WWII, Jim's pursuits in photography continued. He would study cinematography at the University of Southern California and attend business and art school at the University of Colorado, before settling in Medicine Lodge, Kansas.

He married Janet Brosius in 1951, and from that union, two sons were born, Tony and Chris. For the next thirty years (1960–1990), Jim worked in the family-owned General Motors dealership. When Jim retired, he returned to his love of photography. Chris joined him in his work and, together, would spend many hours photographing American landscapes and lifestyles, sharing a mutual passion born of talent and inspiration.

It was during this time that stock agencies were low on photos of Western content. Already having a particular interest in Western photography, the opportunity was a perfect fit for the Bertoglio pair. And so began a work that would span the next decade as Jim and Chris photographed the daily lives of the working cowboy on some of the largest and last-remaining ranches on the Great Plains. In

2005, their stunning photos transformed into an exhibit called The Vanishing Cowboy. Sadly, Jim passed away on October 26, 2012, before his vision for a book of similar content could be realized.

It is my privilege to have become acquainted with the Bertoglio family and to see Jim's dream become a reality. *The Vanishing Cowboy* is a concise story of the American cowboy—icon of the American West—from his origin in the great cattle drives to his present uncertain end. Jim's desire for the book—coupled with beautiful images taken with his son, Chris, and an historical text written by Jim Hoy—helps preserve this rich heritage. Together, they have aspired to keep it from ever vanishing.

—Lois Lenkner
January 2014

INTRODUCTION

The American cowboy, our nation's dominant folk hero and an internationally recognized symbol of our country, had his origin in the great Texas-to-Kansas cattle drives that followed the Civil War. Men (predominantly men—the cowgirl came along a generation after the cowboy made his appearance) had been working livestock from the backs of horses for centuries all over the world, but it was from the trail dust at Abilene, Ellsworth, Newton, Wichita, Caldwell, and Dodge City that this instantly recognizable folk type found its way into the public consciousness.

This was the era of the open range, before barbed wire had made its way onto the Plains but after the railroads began to cross the continent. The cattle industry had long been established in Texas, fostered by both the Spanish government and by missions of the Catholic Church. The herds continued to flourish after Mexico won its independence in 1821 and after the Texas rebellion in 1836. The Mexican peons, who worked with cattle and horses on the big estancias of south Texas, adapted the Spanish war saddle to their needs in handling the wild and cantankerous longhorns. Their sombreros kept the sun from their eyes, and leather chaparajos protected their legs from mesquite thorns while the big rowels of their spurs helped control the wily mustangs they rode. From these vaqueros (literally cow workers), the American cowboy would acquire his clothing, gear, and work methods.

By the time Texas joined the Union in the later 1840s and into the 1850s, Texas longhorn cattle were being marketed to faraway markets. Some were shipped on boats from Galveston or from New Orleans while others were driven overland along the Shawnee Trail through what is now Oklahoma, Arkansas, Kansas, and Missouri to reach markets in Iowa and Illinois. Still others, following the 1848 gold strike in California, were driven across the Southern deserts to satisfy the appetites of hungry miners. But these early ventures were usually of small herds, a few hundred at most, driven by only a few men. All that changed after the Civil War.

During that conflict, not many Texas cattle were being marketed. Cattle were still being tended on the big ranches, but not many were being sold. After all, to the north and west of Texas were states and territories controlled by the Union, which also soon set up effective blockades on the Mississippi River and the Gulf of Mexico while to the south a sovereign nation with plenty of cattle of its own offered no outlet for Texas steers.

After the war ended, cattle were rife in Texas. Joseph McCoy, the man who made Abilene into a cowtown, said that a Texas rancher's wealth was measured in steers: the more he owned, the poorer he was. But those same steers that were worth maybe two dollars a head in Texas could bring up to forty dollars in Chicago. Fortunes were waiting to be made in Texas cattle, and entrepreneurs were not slow to respond. Now, instead of a few score in a herd, thousands made up a drove. A typical trail herd in the cattle-drive era ranged from two thousand to three thousand head. Ten drovers could easily handle a herd this size.

In addition to the cattle, trail drives included a remuda (i.e., a string of horses for the drovers to ride), a cook and chuck wagon, a horse wrangler, and a trail boss. A herd moved slowly, usually about eight or ten miles a day, which allowed the steers plenty of time to graze and gain weight as they traveled north. At night, the cattle spent about ten hours on the bed ground, which is ample time to rest and ruminate. Thus, a good trail boss—provided there were no stampedes, excessive dry drives, or other troubles—would deliver cattle in Kansas that weighed much more than when they had left Texas, despite having walked several hundred miles.

It was the drovers of these trail herds who formed the basis of the image of the great American cowboy. Most of them were young, in their teens or early twenties. When they arrived at a cowtown—such as Abilene or Dodge City—after two to four months on the trail in the company of nothing but cows and other men, they were ready to blow off steam. Typical pay was a dollar a day, all of which was collected at the end of the trail. Journalists in the cowtowns reported the boisterous displays of these colorful trail hands in the saloons and dance halls, and readers back East read the reports avidly.

At roughly the same time, the hero image portrayed in the dime novels of the day evolved from the Daniel Boone woodsman to the Buffalo Bill plainsman, adding further to the popularity of the cowboy figure. And when Buffalo Bill instituted his Wild West show in the early 1880s, he included cowboys performing the two most colorful and most dangerous parts of their job: riding bucking horses and roping longhorn steers. By the late 1880s, rodeo had become established in range country, turning those cowboy working skills into sport. Then right after the turn of the century came Owen Wister's influential and classic novel *The Virginian*, with its romanticized portrayal of the cowboy. At roughly the same time, *The Great Train Robbery* gave birth to the movie cowboy.

The popular-culture cowboys of dime novels and the movies—white-hatted good guys and their nemeses in black hats—bore little resemblance to the often ragged and scruffy real-life ranch cowboy, but the mythic appeal of that hero—combined with the image of the colorful (although utilitarian) attire of the ranch cowboy and the allure and excitement of his horseback work—has created an indelible image in the American psyche: the freedom-loving horseman in a big hat and high-heeled boots who might be rough around the edges but who always stands with the underdog to right the wrongs foisted by the powerful onto the weak.

The open range began to close with the introduction of barbed wire in the 1880s, and by about 1890, the cowboy had changed from a free-drifting herder to a fence rider, from a trail driver to a ranch hand. The old-timers who had ridden the open range and driven longhorns to Dodge City lamented the end of the cowboy way of life. But twenty years later, their replacements—those first fence-riding, windmill-fixing, ranch-hand cowboys—were lamenting the end of the cowboy way of life when automotive vehicles made their way onto the range. A few decades later, the cowboys who had ridden from the barn to the pasture equated the use of pickup trucks with the end of real cowboys: how could you expect a horse to learn anything about cows if you hauled him around in a trailer instead of riding him to the job? Then came the introduction of four-wheelers to the ranch and roundups with helicopters.

Throughout the history of cattle ranching, technological change has forced its way onto the cowboy way of life, and as old-timers lament each change, the cowboy has adapted his approach to his work, still maintaining its essence: horses and cattle. Today, however, a different kind of threat faces the cowboy. It is not technology but changes in land ownership and usage that threatens his way of life. Large ranches get subdivided into smaller and smaller units while urbanization continues its spread into the West. Industrial wind generators destroy the native grass and the landscape that have traditionally underpinned the ranching industry.

Will the cowboy survive this latest onslaught? Or will industrialization and urbanization bring an end to his means of livelihood, leaving only a few relict remnants, a few theme parks to preserve a mere semblance of the cowboy's true life? Let us hope that the cowboy, America's true folk hero, can again adapt to change and emerge with his essence still whole.

The workday of the cowboy begins and ends with the sun. The pay is minimal, but the fringe benefits—riding horses and working cattle amid the grandeur of nature—are priceless.

A Wyoming cowboy and his dog, with the Grand Tetons as a backdrop.

David Ross looks and lives the traditional cowboy life on the Pitchfork Ranch near Guthrie, Texas.

Born with a rope in his hand, this youngster from Syracuse, Kansas,
is learning one of the major cowboy skills early.

Following the wagon: looking like a scene from the 1880s, the remuda and chuck wagon are headed for a roundup on the Pitchfork Ranch. *Remuda*, like many of the words used by cowboys, is of Spanish origin and refers to a herd (or string) of horses.

Glenn and Brian Taylor riding along a pole fence near Jackson Hole, Wyoming.

Kansas cowboy Rex Bugbee and his horse with typical cowboy gear: felt hat, long-sleeved shirt, leather chaps, boots, saddle, breast collar, and bridle.

Swinging a big loop. Not all cowboys are good ropers, but those who are get much enjoyment from this exciting part of the job.

Bringing the horses home near Telluride, Colorado. Despite mechanizations, many ranches still rely on horses for working cattle.

The cowboy boot is both colorful and utilitarian. Cobbler Charles Hyer is credited with making the first pair back in 1875 when a Colorado drover stopped by his shop in Olathe, Kansas, after delivering cattle to the Kansas City stockyards.

The horse is often seen as a mythic symbol of freedom and power. A good horse is the most useful, and cherished, tool the cowboy has.

The general store in the small towns of cattle country—like this one in Belvidere, Kansas—is often the gathering place for local cowboys.

Waggoner Ranch cowboys get their early-morning orders near Vernon, Texas. At the beginning of the day, the cow boss will usually assign each cowboy specific work.

Like many traditional ranches, the Chain Ranch maintains
a string of good quarter horse broodmares.

The cowboy is outlined at sunset in the Gypsum Hills of Barber County, Kansas.

Bison and American Indians, like the ancestors of Kiowa chief Vernon Tosodle of Lawton, Oklahoma, were native to the Plains before cowboys and cattle.

The most important, and often the most colorful, building on a ranch is the barn, like this one near the Snake River and Grand Tetons in Wyoming.

In 1867, a peace treaty between the US government and the Cheyenne, Comanche, Kiowa, Kiowa-Apache, and Arapaho Indians was signed at Medicine Lodge, Kansas, an event commemorated triennially with a pageant.

Pitchfork Ranch horse wrangler moving the remuda to summer camp. Traditionally the wrangler played an important role, making sure that fresh horses were available when needed by the cowboys.

These covered wagons at the Medicine Lodge Peace Treaty Pageant
recall the settlement of the prairie during pioneer times.

Rancher Jim Harbaugh shutting a gate in Barber County, Kansas. Invented in the late 1860s, barbed wire became economically feasible a decade later, and by the 1880s, wire fences were bringing an end to the days of the open range.

A Barber County, Kansas, cowboy shakes out a loop. Along with many other cattle-working skills, the cowboy learned roping from the Mexican vaquero. The lariat rope derives its name from the vaquero's *la reata*.

Two cowboys checking fence on the Chain Ranch. Once the open range had been fenced, riding fence became part of the cowboy's job.

Sorting cattle on the Lee Ranch near San Mateo, New Mexico. Working cattle in a set of pens is often a favorite job if a cowboy is mounted on a good cowhorse.

Cattle on summer pasture near Vail, Colorado. In the mountains cattle graze in the high country in summer, then are fed hay at ranch headquarters in winter.

Tom Mattingly of the Padlock Ranch getting ready to rope at a ranch rodeo in Hardin, Montana.

Three Waggoner Ranch cowboys head for the barn at the end of the day. The long hours of ranch work are eased by the camaraderie among cowboys.

This Padlock Ranch cowboy makes up for an early morning by taking
a nap while waiting for the cattle-hauling trucks to arrive.

Cowboys use many different types of headgear on their horses. Mike Jones of the Chain Ranch is using a mecate (a length of rope used as bridle reins, Anglicized to McCarty) and a bosal (a rawhide hackamore) on his horse.

Jim Bob Glover sorts out a calf for branding on the Waggoner Ranch.
A good cutting horse is highly prized by cowboys.

At spring roundup, one cowboy ropes a calf while a ground crew wrestles it
to the ground for vaccinating, castrating, earmarking, and branding.

The day's work complete, a cowboy leads his horse out of the barn
at the Houlton ranch in Barber County, Kansas.

Pair of working boots on the barn floor on Four Sixes (6666) Ranch, Guthrie, Texas.

Brian Taylor prepares to saddle his horse near Jackson Hole, Wyoming. Cowboys often refer to their saddles as their office, and will sometimes spend two or three months' wages to acquire a good custom-made saddle.

Padlock Ranch cowboys move a herd of cows and calves in Wyoming.
Driving cattle is one of the common chores on a ranch.

At the Medicine Lodge Peace Treaty Pageant, cowboys reenact a trail drive with a herd of longhorns.

A cowboy and a cowgirl from the Pitchfork Ranch share driving as the chuck wagon and remuda move to summer camp.

Rex Bugbee has tied onto a big cow that needs doctoring. A good roping horse is essential to good cowboying.

Rex Bugbee checking cattle in the tall grass of the Chain Ranch. Riding pasture in order to count cattle, look for strays, and doctor sick livestock is part of the normal routine on a ranch.

Bringing a calf to the ground crew on the Waggoner Ranch. Roping a calf by the heels and dragging it to the crew is a favorite job at roundup time, a technique unchanged from the days of the open range.

David Ross bringing in the Pitchfork Ranch remuda.

Mike Sample of Salina prepares to rope at the Kansas Championship Ranch Rodeo, held annually at Medicine Lodge. Contemporary professional rodeo, which originated from the riding and roping skills of the cowboy, has little relevance nowadays to actual ranch work.

A contestant at the Kansas Championship Ranch Rodeo. Ranch rodeo, which began in the 1980s with events based on everyday ranch jobs such as calf branding and cattle sorting, has brought rodeo back to its roots.

Evidence of hard work and a good life show in Jim Packard's face
and in his well-worn saddle, near Lake City, Kansas.

A cowboy and covered wagon at the Medicine Lodge Peace Treaty Pageant.

David Marino of the Waggoner Ranch, with new chaps and a new rope, checks his cinch.

Mike Samples at the Kansas Championship Ranch Rodeo. A good horse and a sure rope are essential tools for the cowboy.

Bridle reins, saddle horn, and Rex Bugbee's hands reflect the hard and sometimes dangerous work of the cowboy.

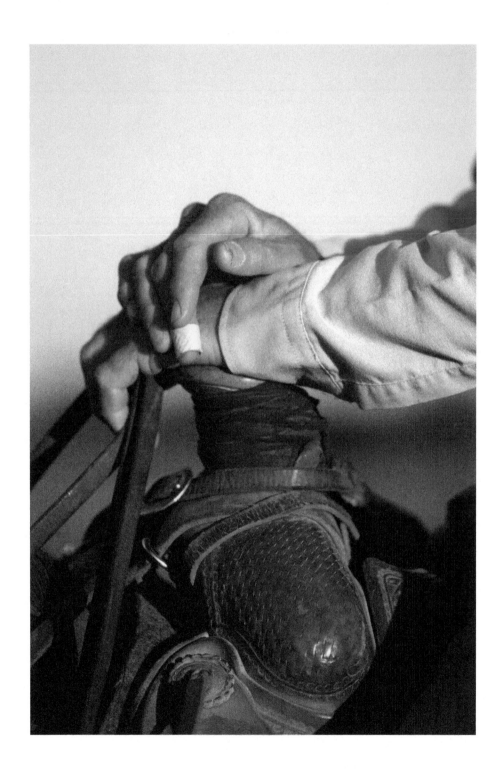

Stirrup, boot, and spur show evidence of hard riding, but not walking. A cowboy will mount a horse to ride from one side of a corral to the other.

Is the American cowboy headed for the sunset?

About the Authors and Photographers

JIM BERTOGLIO received his first formal instruction in photography from the prestigious Art Center School in Los Angeles, where he studied under famed photographer and mentor Ansel Adams. His studies, however, were cut short when he was assigned duty as a military photographer in the US Air Force during World War II. Home again, Jim attended Business and Art School at the University of Colorado, Boulder, and the University of Southern California–Cinematography, Los Angeles, before settling in Medicine Lodge, Kansas, where he resided until his death in 2012. A member of the VFW, Jim traveled to Washington with the Honor Flight of World War II veterans. He is nationally known for his collection of black-and-white WWII photos.

Photo credits: Marlboro, Continental Airlines, *Chicago Tribune*, *Washington Daily News*, Bell Telephone, Air Force books and aviation magazines, Buick Motor Division, Colorado resort publications, *Kansas!* magazine, Kansas tourism magazine, Kansas calendar, *Western Horseman*, *Wichita Eagle*, *Flight* magazine, *Ad Astra* magazine, Emprise Bank, and numerous national and international magazine advertisements.

Showings: Litwin Gallery, Wichita, Kansas; Light Impressions, Rochester, New York; Index Stock Photography, New York, New York; Pratt Junior College, Pratt, Kansas; Colby Junior College, Colby, Kansas; Superstock, Jacksonville, Florida; Kansas Museum of History–Kansas Historical Society, Topeka, Kansas; Kansas State Capitol appropriations room, Topeka, Kansas; Hampton Inn, Dodge City, Kansas; Exploration Place, Wichita, Kansas; Fine Print Imaging (Art for Conservation), Fort Collins, Colorado.

Donated works: Smithsonian Air and Space Museum archive collection and the LA Art Center School.

CHRIS BERTOGLIO, son of late photographer Jim Bertoglio, resides in Medicine Lodge, Kansas, home to the scenic Gypsum Hills. Chris attended the University of Kansas in Lawrence, where he studied marketing and advertising. He later earned his real estate license and practiced for fifteen years. Chris became the third-generation Bertoglio to join the family General Motors dealership before it sold in 1990. He traveled extensively with his father after his retirement and was instrumental in forming Americana Images.

Photo credits: *Kansas!* magazine, Kansas calendar, *Ad Astra* magazine, *Wichita Eagle*, Emprise Bank, and *Texas: An Empire Wide and Glorious* (cover shot; foreword written by former president George Bush Sr.)

Showings: Index Stock Photography, New York, New York; Hampton Inn, Dodge City, Kansas; Superstock, Jacksonville, Florida; Fine Print Imaging (Art for Conservation), Fort Collins, Colorado; Exploration Place, Wichita, Kansas

JIM HOY, reared on a ranch in the Kansas Flint Hills near Cassoday, is a professor of English and director of the Center for Great Plains Studies at Emporia State University, where he has taught since 1970. He holds a BS from Kansas State University, an MA from Emporia State University, and a PhD from the University of Missouri. He is an authority on the folklife of ranching, a topic on which he has lectured in England, Germany, New Zealand, and Australia. Among the books he has published are *The Cattle Guard: Its History and Lore* (University Press of Kansas, 1982); *Cowboys and Kansas* (Oklahoma University Press, 1995); *Vaqueros, Cowboys, and Buckaroos* (University of Texas Press, 2001, with Jerald Underwood and Lawrence Clayton); *Flint Hills Cowboys* (University Press of Kansas, 2006); and *Cowboy's Lament: A Life on the Open Range* (Texas Tech University Press, 2010). He is past president of the Kansas Historical Society and the American Association of Australian Literary Studies and past chair of the Board of Trustees of the American Folklife Center at the Library of Congress. In 2004, he was inducted into the Kansas Cowboy Hall of Fame.

ACKNOWLEDGMENTS

Much gratitude is owed to the ranches that graciously permitted the Bertoglios to photograph on their land and their work.

Chain Ranch, Medicine
    Lodge, KS

Lee Ranch, San Mateo, NM

Waggoner Ranch, Vernon, TX

Four Sixes (6666)
    Ranch, Guthrie, TX

Houlton Ranch, Barber
    County, KS

Padlock Ranch,
    Ranchester, WY

Pitchfork Ranch,
    Guthrie, TX

TECHNICAL NOTES

Jim and Chris Bertoglio used Leica camera and lenses, EOS Canon film cameras, L series 17 mm to 400 mm zoom lenses, and Kodak SW film exclusively. All their film processing was done at Reed Photo, Denver, Colorado. Gallery prints are available through Fine Print Imaging (Art for Conservation), Fort Collins, Colorado. For more information, contact americanaimages@usa.com.

A NOTE OF THANKS

To Lois Lenkner, for rekindling the dream of getting this book into print and then contributing her time and talent to help make it so.

CPSIA information can be obtained
at www.ICGtesting.com
Printed in the USA
BVOW10*1644171016

464956BV00055B/17/P